Oh, No... I have to go...

# FIRST DAY OF SCHOOL

## BY ROSE ANGEBRANDT

with Keigan Voros

Published and written by Rose Angebrandt

ISBN: 978-1-9991187-0-9

Copyright © 2019 by Rose Angebrandt

**www.roseangebrandt.com**

For Keigan and Ayzlin

You are loved more than words can say

Oh, No... I have to go...

... to School. I think I am afraid...

What if I forget the way to walk to School?

What if I cannot find a friend who will play with me?

What if my classroom is hard to find?

What if my Teacher is big and scary?

What if the Teacher asks me a

Question and I give the wrong answer?

What if the other kids in my class laugh at me?

OH, NO... I SHOULD NOT GO!!

Well... I guess... it may be pretty hard

to forget where my school is...

It is so close to my house...

I guess... it should not be too hard to find a friend...

All of the kids on my street go to my School...

Hmmm... There are not that many classrooms. I think it may be ok...

My Teacher is really pretty. She has
a nice smile. I think I like her.

"Do I know how to count to 10? I sure do! I can even count to 20!"

The other kids are clapping and not laughing at me! I like Grade 1! I can do this!

OH, YES... I WANT TO GO AND WILL GO...

... TO SCHOOL!

Hello Readers!

Amazon review can make a huge difference
to the overall success of this Book.

If you enjoyed reading this Book as much as I have enjoyed
writing it, please take a few moments to leave a quick review.

I would really appreciate it!

Thank YOU!

ROSE ANGEBRANDT

Made in the USA
Middletown, DE
26 July 2021